THE DOT and THE LINE

a romance in lower mathematics

by
NORTON
JUSTER

Random
House

Grateful acknowledgment is made to the following for permission
to reprint previously published material:

AMERICAN MUSEUM OF NATURAL HISTORY: Negative number 37126-Spider Web.
Courtesy American Museum of Natural History.
ARTISTS RIGHTS SOCIETY, INC.: *Little Jester in Trance* by Paul Klee.
Copyright © 1990 ARS N.Y./COSMOPRESS. Reprinted by permission of Artist's Rights Society.
BETTMANN ARCHIVES: Negative number P012711-Tug of War and Negative
number PG13131-Euclid Portrait. Reprinted by permission of The Bettmann Archive, New York.
THE METROPOLITAN MUSEUM OF ART: ACC. #37.162, photo of *Venus and Adonis*
by Peter Paul Rubens. Gift of Harry Payne Bingham, 1937.
Reprinted by permission of The Metropolitan Museum of Art.

Manufactured in the United States of America
98765432
Random House, Inc., 1991 edition

For Euclid, no matter what they say.

Once upon a time there was a sensible straight line
who was hopelessly in love

with a dot.

"You're the beginning and the end, the hub, the core and the quintessence," he told her tenderly, but the frivolous dot wasn't a bit interested,

for she only had eyes for a wild and unkempt squiggle
who never seemed to have anything on his mind at all.

They were everywhere together, singing and dancing and frolicking and laughing and laughing and lord knows what else.

"He is so gay and free, so uninhibited and full of joy," she informed the line coolly,

"and you are as stiff as a stick. Dull. Conventional and repressed. Tied and trammeled. Subdued, smothered and stifled. Squashed, squelched and quenched."

"Come around when you get straightened out, kid," the squiggle added with a rasping chuckle, as he chased her into the high grass.

"Why take chances," replied the line without much conviction. "I'm dependable.

I know where I'm going.

I've got dignity!"

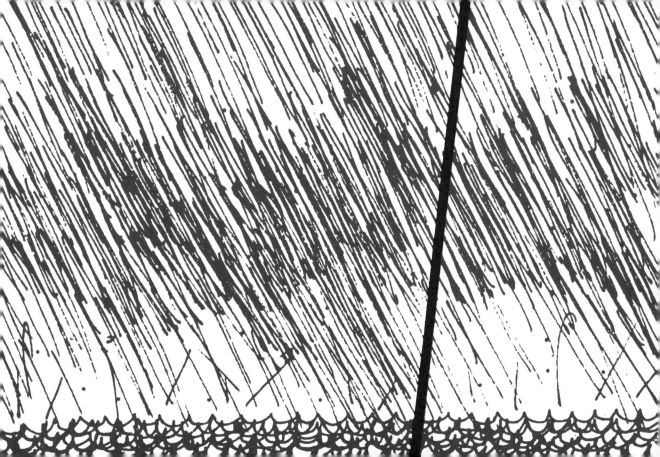

But this was small consolation for the miserable line. Each day he grew more and more morose. He stopped eating or sleeping and before long was completely on edge.

His worried friends noticed how terribly thin and drawn he had become and did their best to cheer him up.

"She's not good enough for you."

"She lacks depth."

"They all look alike anyway. Why don't you find a nice straight line and settle down?"

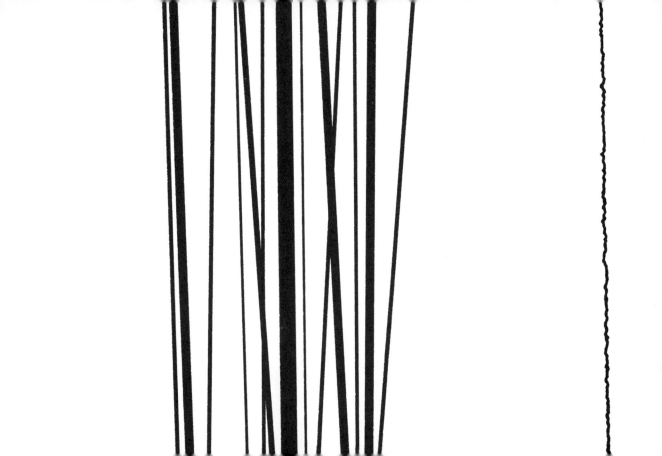

But he hardly heard a word they said. Any way he looked at her she was perfect.

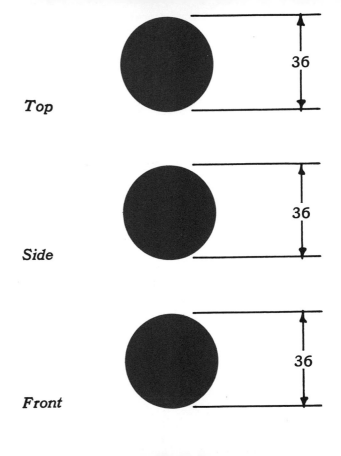

Top

Side

Front

He saw things in her that no one else could possibly imagine.

"She is more beautiful than any straight line I've ever seen," he sighed wistfully, and they all shook their heads. Even allowing for his feelings they felt this was stretching a point.

And so he spent his time dreaming of the inconstant dot and imagining himself as the forceful figure she was sure to admire ——

THE LINE AS A
CELEBRATED DAREDEVIL

THE LINE AS A
LEADER IN WORLD AFFAIRS

THE LINE AS A FEARLESS
LAW ENFORCEMENT AGENT

THE LINE AS A POTENT
FORCE IN THE WORLD OF ART

THE LINE AS AN
INTERNATIONAL SPORTSMAN

But he soon grew tired of self-deception and decided that perhaps the squiggly line might have the answer after all.

"I lack spontaneity. I must learn to let go, to be free, to express the inner passionate me."

But it just didn't make any difference, for no matter how often, or how hard he tried,

he always ended up the same way.

And yet he continued trying and failing and trying again. Until when he had all but given up, he discovered at last that with great concentration and self-control he was able to change direction and bend wherever he chose. So he did, and made an angle.

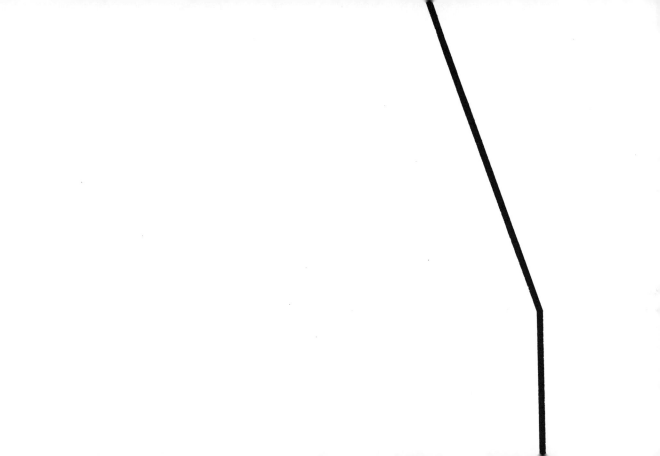

And then again and made another

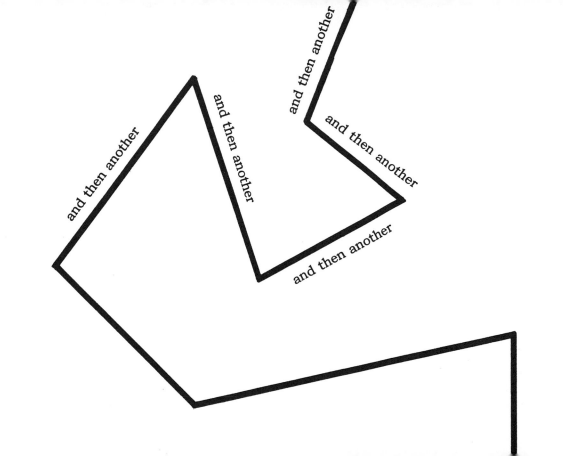

"Hot stuff," he shouted, much impressed with his efforts. Then in a wild burst of enthusiasm he sat up for half the night putting on an outrageous display of sides, bends and angles.

"Freedom is not a license for chaos," he observed the next morning. "Ooh, what a head." There and then he decided not to squander his talents in cheap exhibitionism.

For months he practiced in secret. Soon he was making squares and triangles, hexagons, parallelograms, rhomboids, polyhedrons, trapezoids, parallelepipeds, decagons, tetragrams and an infinite number of other shapes so complex that he had to letter his sides and angles to keep his place.

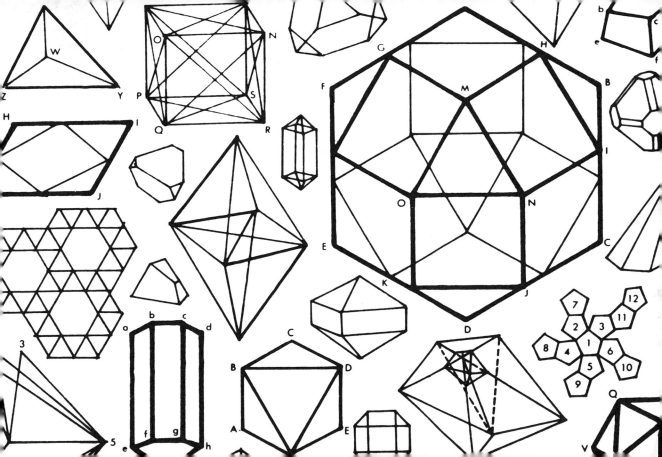

Before long he had learned to carefully control ellipses, circles and complex curves and to express himself in any shape he wished —

"You name it, I'll play it."

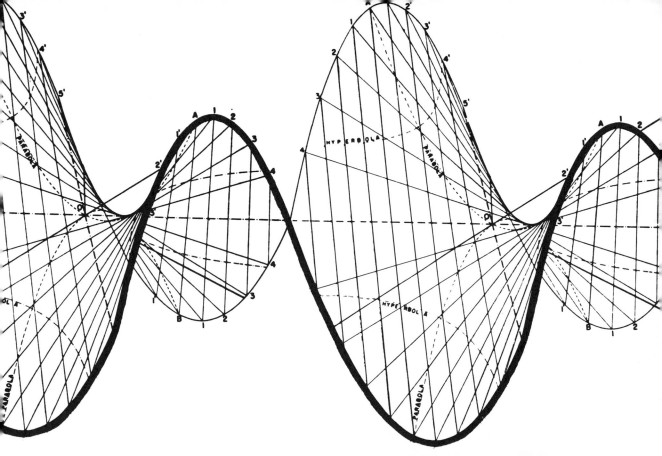

But all his successes meant nothing to him alone and so off he went to seek the dot once again.

"He doesn't stand a chance," muttered the squiggle in a voice that sounded like bad plumbing.

But the line, who was bursting with old love and new confidence, was not to be denied. Throughout the evening he was by turns —

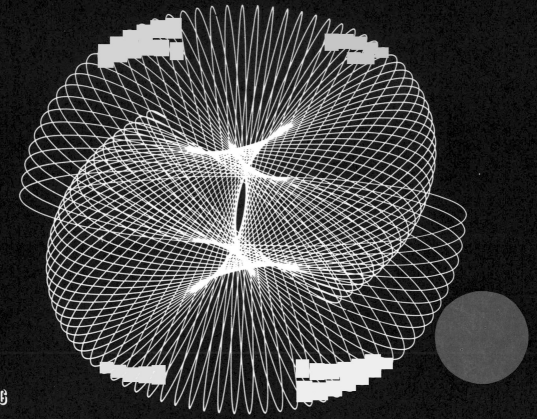

DAZZLING

Clever

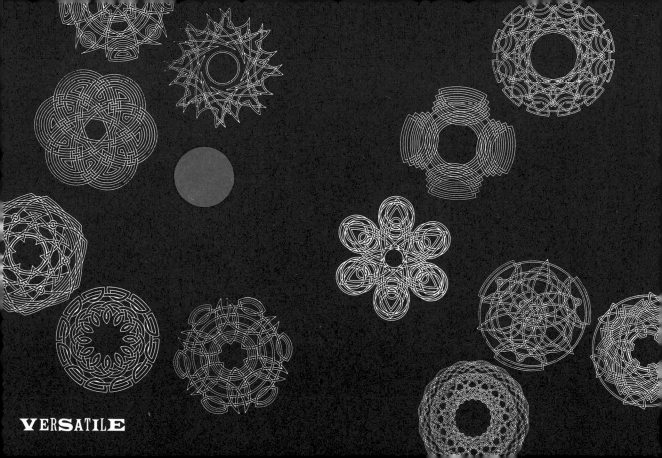

VERSATILE

ERUDITE

Eloquent

PROFOUND

ENIGMATIC

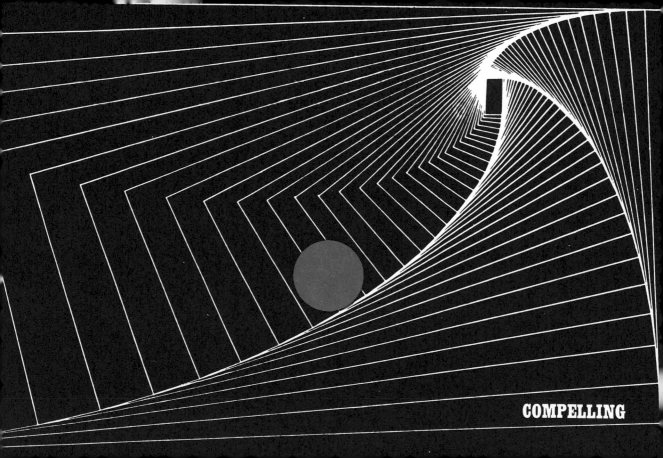

COMPELLING

The dot was overwhelmed. She giggled like a school-girl and didn't know what to do with her hands. Then she turned slowly to the squiggle, who had suddenly developed a severe cramp.

"Well?" she inquired, trying to give him every chance.

The squiggle, taken by surprise, did the best he could.

"Is that all?" she demanded.

"I guess so," replied the miserable squiggle. "That is, I suppose so. What I mean is I never know how it's going to turn out. Hey, have you heard the one about the two guys who —"

The dot wondered why she had never noticed how hairy and coarse he was, and how untidy and graceless, and how he mispronounced his L's and picked his ear.

And suddenly she realized that what she had thought was freedom and joy was nothing but anarchy and sloth.

"You are as meaningless as a melon," she said coldly. "Undisciplined, unkempt and unaccountable, insignificant, indeterminate and inadvertent, out of shape, out of order, out of place and out of luck."

With that she turned to the line and shyly took his arm.

"Do the one with all the funny curves again, honey," she cooed softly as they strolled away.

And he did.

And soon they did, and lived ——

if not happily ever after, at least reasonably so

Moral: To the vector belong the spoils.

Acknowledgments

Cover Drawing — *George Paul Schmidt, Jr.*
Tug of War — *The Bettmann Archive*
Euclid — *The Bettmann Archive*
Circus and Traffic scenes — *U.P.I.*
Rubens: Venus and Adonis — *The Metropolitan Museum of Art,*
Gift of Harry Payne Bingham,
1937
Cosmograph — *Photo-Lettering*
Klee: Little Jester in Trance — *The Thinking Eye,* by Paul Klee,
The Documents of Modern Art
Series, Vol. 15, published by
George Wittenborn, Inc., 1961;
© by S.P.A.D.E.M., Paris, 1977.
Spider Web — *Courtesy of the American Museum*
of Natural History
Diagrams: "Compelling" — *Scripta Mathematica*
"Complex" — *Scripta Mathematica*
"Enigmatic" — *Scripta Mathematica*

8/12•8 Bookman w/Italic 8.5d
9 Bookman w/Italic 9.5d

NORTON JUSTER, a practicing architect, lives in Buckland, Massachusetts, and teaches at Hampshire College. This is his second book. His first, *The Phantom Tollbooth*, has already established itself as a children's classic and, in the tradition of *Alice* and *Gulliver*, as an adult delight as well. He has been accused of writing on several levels and appealing to a suspiciously wide audience. THE DOT AND THE LINE is a mathematical fable. It is for readers of all ages from dark to middle.